the PRAYER principle
by Jim Graham

CONTENTS

Cover design: Ross Advertising and Design Limited ·
Designer: Paul Edwards · Inside illustrations: Paulo Baigent ·
Typeset by HWTypesetters, Norwich · Printed by Ebenezer Baylis & Son
Limited, The Trinity Press, Worcester and London ·
© Scripture Union 1994, 130 City Road, London EC1V 2NJ·ISBN 086201 819 6

Many years ago, I visited a home in Greenock on the west coast of Scotland. Having met the parents, I was introduced to the daughter of the family, a young woman of about 30 years of age, well-dressed and well-groomed. However, she was sitting on the floor playing with a doll. Very soon I realised, that although she had an adult's body, her mind was that of a little child.

It didn't take long to discover that this girl, so deeply loved by her parents, was also the cause of great sadness and hurt in their hearts. For this daughter had failed to grow and develop as they – and everybody else – would have expected.

That's how our heavenly Father must feel about some of us – physically and mentally there has been growth and development, yet spiritually we remain immature and stunted. Since you probably feel the need to grow in Jesus, that, perhaps, is why you have bought this book. Well, be patient, like physical growth, spiritual growth is quite slow, and impossible to measure on a daily basis. However, over a period of time, although you may feel you are not where you should like to be spiritually, nevertheless, you are certainly not where you used to be.

ANSWERS NEEDED

This book doesn't promise instant and dramatic results, though, used properly, it will encourage growth in your relationship with God. But there are some questions that need to be answered before you proceed any further:

● Do I really want to hear God speak to me?

● Am I really willing to persevere until

I hear God speak to me more often/ clearly?

● Is there a desire in my heart to please God?

● Am I concerned to do something about my personal spiritual growth and development?

● Do I need to discipline my will and to make a new beginning now?

● Do I really expect a response from God?

● Am I willing to set aside time not just to read what is written but to 'relax' before God?

Take time as you read this book to return to these questions and give some honest answers.

MAKE ROOM FOR GOD

The way we use our time can either be a great asset or a great hindrance to our growth with Jesus.

The Twenty-Third Psalm for Busy People – a preface to World Vision's manual on Time Management – expresses the difference to life when we are prepared to make room for God:

> The Lord is my pace-setter, I shall not rush, He makes me stop and rest for quiet intervals, He provides me with images of stillness, which restore my serenity.
> He leads me in ways of effectiveness through calmness of mind, and His guidance is peace.
> Even though I have a great many things to accomplish today, I will not fret for His presence is here.
> His timelessness, His all-importance will keep me in balance.
> He prepares refreshment and renewal in the midst of my

activity by anointing my mind
with his oils of tranquility,
My cup of joyous energy
overflows.
Surely harmony and effectiveness
shall be the fruit of my hours,
for I shall walk at the pace of
my Lord, and dwell in His
house forever.

PRAYER LINK

We need to 'unwind' in the presence
of God.

He wants to listen to *me* when I
speak to him and he wants me to listen
to *him* when he speaks to me. I am
never out of his mind. He cares for me.
He loves me more than I love myself. He
accepts me as I am and is changing me
to be like him.

You will find it helpful to pray before
and after you read the Bible. One of
these two outlines might act as a guide:

1 Think of *sorry, thank you, please...*

● A *sorry* prayer – confessing your sin
to God.

● A *thank you* prayer – thanking God
for some blessing or answered prayer.

● A *please* prayer – asking the Lord to
meet some particular need in your life.

2 Think of the word *ACTS*. That stands
for:

Adoration – worship and praise God
for who he is.

Confession – admitting failure and
asking for forgiveness.

Thanksgiving – thanking God for what
he has done.

Supplication – praying for other people or for yourself.

As you use one of these outlines your
prayer life will begin to grow.

GROWING WITH OTHERS

You will find it helpful to tell another
mature Christian that you are starting to
use this book. Then get together from
time to time to talk about what you are
learning and how it is affecting you.

We are using the *New International
Version* of the Bible. Like all trans-
lations, it has its limitations. Nevertheless it will lead you to a fuller
understanding of what the Bible says,
and, even more importantly, to encounters with the living Lord Jesus
Christ.

Each set of readings is introduced by
an article that includes more about the
following theme. It also grapples with
some of the knotty problems that come
up in the Bible verses. Then the extras
at the end of each series will help
you delve a little more into the Bible's
teaching on prayer.

With the Bible open, this book open,
a notebook and pencil, let's go!

the
prayer
principle

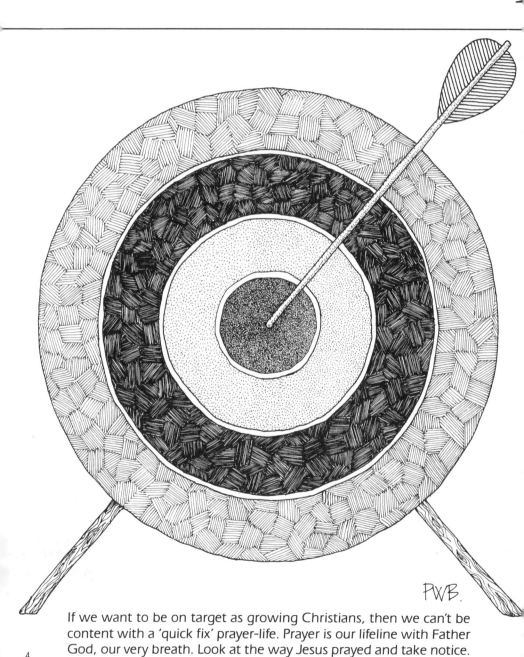

PWB.

If we want to be on target as growing Christians, then we can't be content with a 'quick fix' prayer-life. Prayer is our lifeline with Father God, our very breath. Look at the way Jesus prayed and take notice.

ight on target

Prayer is the Christian's ballistic missile - one which hits its target every time. There is no defence against it. It travels at the speed of thought, is fuelled by faith, is equipped with a delayed detonation mechanism, and it obliterates the limitations of space and time.

Jesus, the Son of God, but human like us, was much more aware of the significance of prayer than we are. When he faced conflict and difficult decisions; when he found himself in a crisis and knew that the moment was crucial; when his heart overflowed with emotion; when his days were crowded and busy; when he wanted God to demonstrate his power - he prayed!

The first Christians followed Jesus' example and did the same thing - they prayed - at night and in the morning; in the storm and the calm; in prison and on the seashore; when they were persecuted and when they were dying; when they appointed leaders; and when new Christians joined them. Prayer was like the air they breathed - a vital life-support system for effective Christian living.

EXPECT ANSWERS

Ever since, anyone who has proved effective in society and for the kingdom of God has only been successful *with* prayer. Think about George Muller of Bristol. His society cared for 10,000 orphans over a period of 60 years, receiving more than £2 million in the process. He began with only two shillings (10p) in his pocket, and without once asking for money he received enough to build five large children's homes and feed his extended family day-by-day. All this by faith and prayer! Before starting any project, Muller always first made sure

he was doing God's will. He knew God's heart was towards children and the disadvantaged; he shared his concerns with one or two close friends who confirmed his intentions and checked his motives; and he had an inner security that God was giving him the go-ahead. Then, taking hold of God's promises in the Bible, boldly he came to him in prayer. No delay discouraged him. Once persuaded a thing was right, he kept praying until the answer came.

A stickler for detail, he kept a complete record of his prayers. It covered 3,000 pages, contained nearly a million words, and listed more than 50,000 specific answers.

GET YOUR ACT TOGETHER

Everything around us shouts: 'Don't just sit there, *do* something!' But sometimes the heart-felt cry from God is, 'Don't just do something, *sit* there!' Nobody has made a deeper impression on history than Jesus - and he certainly didn't hang about. But there was an impressive balance in his life between *doing* and *praying*. He spent whole nights in prayer, and yet when faced with a person in need, he acted with speed and authority. So for him prayer took hours and ministry minutes. All too often our activity is just the reverse.

Jesus knew that prayer is the way we can get what God wants to give. If

the
prayer
principle

we feel we are missing out in our experience, in our lives, and in our work, then the secret is *more* prayer (James 4:2, 3). Prayer is the means God has appointed for us to receive forgiveness and Father's sheer undeserved generous help in times of need (Hebrews 4:16). Fullness of joy (Psalm 16:11; John 16:24) and the reality of the fullness of the Holy Spirit (Luke 11:13; Acts 4:31; 8:15) are *both* obtained by prayer. Freedom from anxiety and entrance into the peace of God is discovered as we accept and walk the pathway of prayer (Philippians 4:6, 7): *please,* do look at thèse Bible references!

the prayer principle

CHANGE OF PERSPECTIVE

Prayer is not so much *me* bringing God into *my* world to solve *my* problems as it is *God* bringing me into *his* world to serve *his* purposes. Prayer gives a totally different perspective to my life. It is a God-centred exercise.

In one night in history the whole pattern of prayer was changed. It was the night before Jesus was crucified. Five times on that great occasion, Jesus said, 'Use my name when you pray' (John 14:13, 14; 15:16; 16:23, 24). When you use someone's name as a guarantee, you are aware you are doing something, or saying something, of which he would approve. God wants us to have what Jesus wants for us. Our Lord and Master, Jesus, spent a lot of time putting his earthly life in God's divine perspective – and we need to do this too.

When Jesus prayed, all hell was set loose. His praying seems to have released a whole torrent of spiritual hostility. For Jesus, 'let the battle commence' seems as good a description of his praying as anything else. Jesus confronted profoundly disturbing encounters with evil in prayer (eg Matthew chapter 4 and Luke chapter 22). So must we. Prayer is a key piece of armour in our battle against demonic forces. One of the things we need to guard against as Christians is thinking of ourselves as civilians living in peace-time, when in fact we are soldiers living in wartime.

If being a Christian is living the Jesus-life in the power of the Holy Spirit – and it is – then we need to realise the prime importance of prayer as it was for Jesus. In Mark's Gospel, our first encounter with Jesus is in Capernaum, watching him heal the sick and set people free from dark, demonic powers. No doubt it left him feeling physically, emotionally and spiritually exhausted and in need of rest. But then we see his secret for spiritual refreshment – 'very early in the morning. . . Jesus got up, left the house and went off to a solitary place, where he prayed' (Mark 1:35). In that moment the disciples witnessed the link between prayer and power – but missed the point of it.

So, in order to meet the poverty of our own lives, have God's perspective on life, confront demonic powers and be effective in service, we need to pray. Let us walk through the next few days together learning all we can from the way Jesus lived and communed with his Father.

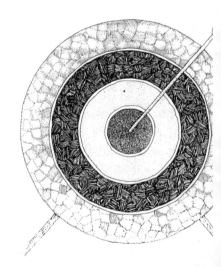

Right on target

Day 1
BEGINNING AND BATTLES
Luke 3:21, 22; 4:1-13

It was spring 1809 in Scotland. Storekeeper, Neil Livingstone had two brothers at the front in Europe with the Duke of Wellington. Napoleon had faced his military disaster in Moscow. Down on the corner of a Blantyre street, a group of men waited impatiently for the lumbering old stage-coach to bring news from the war. Europe was getting ready for Waterloo. It was all pretty heady stuff – without a radio or a telly! But a baby's cry penetrated the tense conversation of the men who talked about national and international events and about life and death – David Livingstone was born! That little baby was to open Africa up as explorer, emancipator and evangelist. That new beginning had a greater effect on the world than the battles of the Peninsular War with Wellington and Soult.

Here a new beginning is being made (3:21, 22) – not by a baby, but by a man who is God. Heaven is opened by prayer, and resources and assurance are secured by prayer. So Jesus is able to confront the real enemy (4:1-12) and win a decisive battle (4:13).

Prayer starter:
Lord, help me to make a new beginning today. Enable me to receive what you want to give me, and hear what you want to say to me, so that I too can confront temptation and win.

Day 2
CHOICES TO BE MADE
Luke 6:12-16

Today, you will make many choices – some without thinking; others after serious thought; some which don't really matter, and others that will, perhaps, affect our future. Some choices are made for us, but others very definitely have to be made by us.

Jesus is aware in these Bible verses that the purposes of God will be affected by the choices he makes. I'm impressed that he spent a long time praying (v 12) and a very short time choosing (vs 13-16). For our part, we agonise over choosing; Jesus agonised over praying. The result is now church history and present blessing for us. Friends and companions were needed to share his life on earth, but they also had another role – to extend and continue God's work.

Maybe Jesus was surprised at the directions his Father gave him. By any human standards these men left a lot to be desired. The two things that distinguish them were that they were all very different, yet ordinary men. We need to grasp the fact that God doesn't call extraordinary people to do extraordinary things, he calls ordinary people to to ordinary things in an extraordinary way, in the power of his Spirit.

Prayer starter:
Lord, help me not to postpone the choices I need to make because I am afraid of the consequences. Give me time today to bring these choices to you. Help me to hear clearly what you are saying – and then to do what you tell me.

the
prayer
principle

Day 3
IDENTITY CRISIS
Luke 9:18-27

the
prayer
principle

Occasionally, I see in our community one of the weathermen, or an actor, or an entertainer, who appears on television. Immediately I think of them in their TV role, rather than as a real person out shopping. I sometimes wonder if they also have an identity crisis!

Here, Jesus is praying and his Father has been impressing on him who he is – God constantly does this as we pray. Jesus has just accomplished one of his best known and perhaps one of his greatest miracles (vs 10-17). His mind could have been filled with what he had done, but it wasn't (v 18). And there is always the danger of being identified by what we do rather than by what we are. In fact, for those of us today who are unemployed this can be disastrous not only economically but also psychologically – we lose sight of who we are.

So today, in prayer, God wants to impress on us *who* we are – a person in God's heart long before he created the world; born at his time regardless of the physical circumstances of our birth; watched over and cared for by him from the beginning; brought into his family by his grace; created and redeemed for a special function on his agenda; equipped with resources to accomplish all he intended. Secure in who we are, we can face the future regardless of its pain or problems (vs 21-25).

Prayer starter:
Father, show me that I am secure in your love, not because I am loveable, but because you love me.

Day 4
TOO WONDERFUL FOR WORDS
Luke 9:28-36

There is something special about having friends who pray with us. Take time to find one or two who will pray with you on a regular basis. Peter, James and John were the original prayer triplet (v 28). There is a sense in which, even when praying alone, we are never lonely. God, our Father, is attentive; the Holy Spirit is supportive; the hosts of heaven are alerted; and the demons of hell are disturbed and alarmed. This is the way prayer works. But often it is good to have human, physical company sharing in our praying. Sadly, Jesus' prayer companions didn't live up to his expectations and almost missed out (v 32).

There is something else here we should notice – prayer opens heaven and shows us a realm of reality we could so easily miss (vs 29-31). We live in such a self-centred, possession-orientated world. Prayer releases us to see and be part of a reality which is eternal, unseen, and supernatural, as well as historical, seen, and tangible. In prayer, the eternal touches the historical, and the unseen, the seen! Prayer is the road into this divine dimension – not to satisfy our curiosity, but to affirm the purpose and calling of God upon our lives.

Prayer starter:
Lord, help me to find people who will pray with me, so that together we might make discoveries of realities we never knew existed before.

Day 5
SURPRISED BY JOY
Luke 10:21-24

Things had been a bit rough for Jesus (9:46-62) and he might well have felt that anything could happen. The fact that his disciples had come back exhilarated must have been a great relief (vs 1-20). However, it doesn't seem to be his external circumstances which filled Jesus with joy, but the Holy Spirit (vs 21, 22).

Richard Wurmbrand, a Romanian pastor persecuted for his faith, exclaimed, 'I have seen Christians in communist prisons with fifty pounds of chains on their feet, tortured with red hot iron pokers, in whose throats spoonfuls of salt have been forced without water, starving, whipped, suffering from cold and praying with fervour (*and joy*) for the communists. This is humanly inexplicable! It is the love of Christ which was shed into our hearts by the Holy Spirit.'

External problems and internal pressure can often make us feel depressed. As we turn to God in prayer, thanking him for the good things that are happening rather than brooding on the things that aren't, and seeing him at work in *his* way rather than *our* way, we will find that the Holy Spirit will surprise us, too, with joy. God wants to fill us with joy, even though everything around us seems pretty miserable. This is not escapism or fantasy, but reality: reality based on belief that this is God's world and he is in control.

Prayer starter:
Ask the Holy Spirit today not to give you joy, but a new awareness of who God is and what he does.

Day 6
EXPERIENCE COUNTS
Luke 11:1-13

It doesn't really matter whether it's driving a car, cooking a meal, flying an aeroplane, or building a wall – experience counts. There is just no substitute for it. That's why we've been looking at Jesus to learn about praying – he not only spent a lot of time doing it, he knew *how* to do it.

Although we call this 'the Lord's Prayer', it is really the 'Disciples Prayer'. It's short, yet still impressive, because it's not the length of time we spend on prayer that is of first importance (*although most of us don't spend as much time as we should*), but the attitude we have and the content of our dialogue with God.

Jesus says: 'First of all, I get God into perspective when I pray!' (v 2). The most important thing of all is that we realise just who it is we are speaking to. The God to whom we pray is warmly committed to us: wholly different from us, and totally intrusive into our lives. We can bring our needs with confidence before him – our physical, material needs; our spiritual, relationship needs; and our emotional, psychological needs.

Jesus goes on to say: 'Make sure you mean business when you are praying' (vs 5-12). Be assured this is the kind of praying God pays attention to.

Prayer starter:
Lord, I'm grateful that you know I have a lot to learn when it comes to speaking and listening to you. Please help me to learn quickly.

the prayer principle

Reflections

COMPLETE the following as you reflect on what we have shared together so far:

I had never realised that —————

———————————————

———————————————

I am truly sorry that —————————

———————————————

———————————————

One thing I plan to do immediately is

———————————————

———————————————

———————————————

READ Jeremiah 33:3: 'Call to me and I will answer you and tell you great and unsearchable things you do not know.'

THINK:
- Prayer is God's idea not ours.
- Nowhere am I more human than when I pray – animals don't pray!
- Again and again the Bible teaches that God is willing and ready to answer those who will turn to him in believing faith.
- The impossible can become a reality because God is God.

THINK FURTHER: Look up and think about Psalm 50:15, Isaiah 48:6b, Isaiah 55:6, 7.

extra

Day 7
PRAYING FOR OTHERS
John 17:1-26

Shortly before his death, the late King George VI was at Sandringham. His valet took him morning tea, but received no reply to his knock on the bedroom door. After a short interval, he returned – but still no reply. He did this a third time, and became so alarmed at the lack of response that he opened the door. Fearing the worst, he was unprepared for what he saw – the king on his knees in prayer. Embarrassed, he quietly withdrew. He went, a fourth time, and heard the king's invitation to come in. His majesty said: 'Did you knock previously and come in?' 'Yes, sir,' replied the valet. 'If ever you find me on my knees in prayer again,' the King said, 'come and join me!'

We have just read of an infinitely more precious and intimate moment – the King of Kings in prayer. Jesus prays for himself and his own personal situation (vs 1-5). He then goes on to pray for his friends and followers (vs 6-19). Finally, he prays into the future for those who are yet to follow him (vs 20-26).

This is a good pattern for our praying – that God's will may be done and his glory seen in our own lives, in the lives of those around us because of our witness, and on into the lives of future Christians, long after we have gone.

Prayer starter:
Father, help me when I'm praying to be as open, honest and direct as Jesus was. He spent so much more time praying for others than for himself – help me to do the same.

Right on target

Prayer
Test Certificate

The person in question | Christian Yourname |

having been examined under God's prayer laws, it is hereby certified that at the date of examination thereof the statutory requirements prescribed were complied with in relation to communication with Father God.

Signature of tester/inspector | Jesus Christ |

Name in BLOCK CAPITALS | JESUS CHRIST |

Authentication Stamp

WARNING
A Prayer Test Certificate should not be accepted as evidence of the continuing satisfactory nature of the holder's communication with God. The holder's daily life and witness should at all times further endorse his/her competence in the vital exercise of prayer.

ORDER OF
FSH
THE TRINITY

PWB.

Passing the MOG prayer test calls for a great deal of persistence. There's plenty of hard work ahead if we are to surmount the many tricky obstacles that hinder the path to success.

Hindr

Driving through west London, a church poster caught my eye: 'Seven prayerless days make one weak!' Fair enough, if you like that kind of thing, but it is a reminder that praying and spiritual growth go together. Samuel Chadwick, a godly Methodist once said: 'Satan dreads nothing but prayer. His one concern is to keep the saints from praying. He fears nothing from prayerless studies, prayerless work, prayerless religion. He laughs at our toil, mocks our wisdom, but trembles when we pray.'

Pray Test

The person in question Christia having bee laws, it is date of ex requiremen in relation

Signature c

the prayer principle

You see, it's not just a matter of carelessness, but a basic spiritual battle when it comes to making time to pray. There's another saying that goes: 'Satan trembles when he sees the weakest saint upon his knees.' The devil is much more aware of the importance of prayer than we are! He'll do his best to make sure we're too tired, too busy, too frustrated, or too anything to pray. It doesn't matter if we push ourselves to do other things – but not prayer! Even so, we need to be careful and avoid glibly blaming our prayerlessness on satanic activity, real though it undoubtedly is.

CHECK IT OUT

When experiencing difficulty in praying, it helps to go through a check-list.

1 Ask: *'Am I in a right relationship with God?'*

There are *two* ways in which this relationship can be spoiled.

● We can be sinning against God in attitude (*our feelings about him are wrong*). For instance, when we allow the problems and pressures of life to make us resentful and critical of God – 'I don't deserve to suffer like this or to be put in this position!' 'God clearly doesn't love me or even care about

me!' So we stop regarding God as father and friend and see him as a remote and disinterested tyrant.

● We can be sinning against God in action, consciously and deliberately doing something he doesn't approve of, or holding on to something about which he has said 'no' – and so our actions earn his disapproval.

If you are beginning to have problems because you feel your prayers are not being answered, may I suggest a prayer which will get you an answer in moments: 'Lord, show me something in my life which you do not like!' You will be astonished how quickly you get a reply because God wants *everything* to be right between you.

Wrong attitudes always spoil our relationship with our heavenly Father and hinder prayer.

2 Ask: *'Am I in a right relationship with others?'*

There are *two* ways in which we can be in a wrong relationship with other people.

● We can stubbornly refuse to forgive *them* for something they have done.

● Or they can stubbornly refuse to forgive *us* for something we have done to them.

nces to prayer

In both cases, there's the need to put things right so that our prayers aren't hindered. The need for a forgiving attitude is included in the Lord's prayer '…forgive us…as we also have forgiven'. But other people's attitudes can also cause a blockage (Matthew 5:23, 24). Again, it is down to us to work at removing this hindrance.

3 Ask: *'Are we in a right relation with ourselves?'*

It's extraordinary, but God shows us a very simple thing. Getting down on our knees doesn't change us; I am the same person *after* I start praying as I was before.

For example, if we are physically exhausted and emotionally frustrated, or finding it difficult to concentrate on anything, or struggling with disciplining our will generally, then our prayers will surely be affected. Prayer and daily living are integrated. Of course, as we begin to pray the general situation of our lives will be affected, but the general situation of our lives can also affect our praying. A hindrance to prayer need not be caused by a spiritual problem – the cause can be general. For example, maybe the best thing we can do in certain circumstances before praying is to have a good night's sleep.

It's sometimes helpful to pray: 'God, if the problem in my praying lies in one of these three things, then please show me.' Only after exploring along the lines of the three points above can we move on.

4 *'Is the devil fighting and opposing us?'*

We need to give attention to the first three before asking question four, because all too often we blame the devil for things over which he has little responsibility. However, there is a battle going on in heavenly places – unseen by us – which does affect our praying.

For example, on one occasion when Daniel in the Old Testament was praying, the answer was delayed for some time until God's angels had beaten Satan's (Daniel 10:1-21). Spiritual warfare disrupts communication. When we are aware of this, it's time to pray positively against Satan, to claim the protection and power of the blood of Jesus, resisting the devil, and using the power of Jesus' name against him.

There is a fifth question to consider:
5 *'Is God delaying the replies to our prayers because there is something for us to learn?'*

Ask this final question when you are sure you are right with him, with others, and with yourself, and when you have resisted Satan. A 'wait' answer shouldn't weaken your trust in his love and concern for you, whether you feel his presence or not. He wants you to love him for his own sake, and to rejoice in his personal care in every area of your life.

Incidentally, one of the most crippling things in hindering prayer is to wait until we 'feel' God is listening and involved. Nowhere in the Bible are we encouraged to wait for a feeling of God's presence.

Getting hold of the answers to these five important questions will revolutionise our prayers. We need to take time and work at them with determination and honesty.

the
prayer
principle

Day 8
HORIZONTAL HINDRANCE
Matthew 5:21-26

the
prayer
principle

My attitudes to others will always affect my relationship to God – the horizontal affects the vertical.

It's interesting that before Jesus speaks about adultery (vs 27-30), divorce (vs 31, 32), making vows (vs 33-37), and revenge (vs 38-42), he speaks about relationships which affect our contact with God. If you are struggling with prayer today, ask: 'Is everything all right in my relationships with others?'

When Leonardo da Vinci was painting his picture of the Last Supper, he gave Judas the features of a man he hated. It seemed at that moment his genius dried up – the bitterness and resentment he felt poisoned his artistic ability. It was only when he painted out these familiar features that his skill returned. Jesus is teaching here that our anger and insults towards others affect more than just our actions. They also nullify the reality of our relationship with God.

The anger he speaks of is a brooding, inveterate resentment which refuses to die. The verbal insult (v 22) is a word of contempt and loathing. So, it is not only how a man feels towards someone that Jesus corrects, but the way a man speaks.

Prayer starter:
Lord, watch over my feelings and help me to come quickly to you for help when I harbour bad attitudes against another.

Day 9
RIGHT THING: WRONG MOTIVE
Matthew 6:5-15

Moral standards and purity are to be *seen* (5:14, 16), but our close intimate relationship with God is to be *secret*. It is easy to do the right thing for the wrong motive – like giving (vs 1-4); praying (vs 5-15); and fasting (vs 16-18). The secret of true religion is to make sure it's strong on the 'inside', so that it will show on the 'outside'.

To know real vibrancy in prayer, we need to ask: 'Do I really want to meet with God, or am I trying to impress others?' The Jewish system of prayer made 'showing-off' very easy. The Jews prayed standing up with hands stretched out, palms upward, and heads bowed. Prayers had to be said three times a day, wherever a man might be. So it was easy to make sure that at these times you were on a busy street corner, for the world to see your devotion. 'God', says Jesus, 'is unimpressed'.

Of course, it is always helpful to pray with others, but beware of the temptation of trying to compete with or impress them.

Hypocrisy closes heaven and keeps prayer earth-bound – so does unforgiveness (vs 12, 14, 15). We need to be careful in our praying for fear that an unhealed breach, an unsettled quarrel, a resisted opportunity to put things right invites God *not* to forgive us. Our forgiveness of others and God's forgiveness of us are linked and interdependent.

Prayer starter:
Lord, when I come to pray, may I want nothing more, or less, than to meet with you.

Hindrances to prayer

Day 10
LACK OF FAITH
Matthew 21:18-22

The fig tree can be a very imposing tree – some fifteen to twenty feet high, with a three foot thick trunk. Its spread of around thirty feet means it is valued for shade as well as fruit.

Jesus used such a tree as a visual aid to teach that foliage without fruit, show without substance, profession without practice are all useless and invite disaster.

The disciples are astounded by the suddenness, as well as the completeness, of the tree's disintegration (v 20). Jesus uses the incident and their amazement to teach them the need for faith in prayer.

What is faith? It is the sixth sense which enables us to grasp the invisible, but very real, spiritual realm. It is the open hand by which we take what God is offering, not because we deserve it but because he loves us. It is confidence in a God who is absolutely trustworthy and utterly reliable. It is the willingness to accept what we cannot understand. It enables us to discover what God is able to do in the face of all opposition and difficulties. Its chief aim is to obtain the promises of God.

Prayer reflection:
Unbelief says: some other time, but not now; some other person, but not me. *Faith* says: anything God did anywhere else, he will do here; anything he did at any other time, he is willing to do now; anything he did for other people, he is willing to do for me.

Day 11
SPIRITUAL ANSAFONE
Luke 18:9-14

I hate answering-machines because they don't answer – you say what you have to say and that's it!

That's what this is about! Two men in the same place, at the same time, doing the same thing. Yet one gets through in prayer and the other doesn't. The one who fails is good not bad, but proud of his goodness. There's a lot of 'me' in his prayer (*the personal pronoun 'I' occurs six times in two verses*). He tells the truth, but not the *whole* truth. Both of these things need looking at when we're praying. However, the big hindrance is that his prayer doesn't require an answer. Basically, he is congratulating himself on his own performance, and God seems a bit unnecessary.

The other man, who touches God in prayer, could well have been a conscientious worker; a good provider for his family; a loving husband and father. However, he obviously feels awkward and out of place in the presence of God (*not surprising if we really get a hold of what God is like and what we are like*). He actually feels God has never had to handle someone like him ever before (v 13). You would think that would have kept him back, but it doesn't, *nor should it.*

Prayer reflection:
Penitence, not pride, gets answers from God.

the
prayer
principle

Hindrances to prayer

15

Day 12
DOUBT YOUR DOUBTS
James 1:2-8

the
prayer
principle

Earlier this century, a great Christian leader, John R Mott, was shattered by deep doubts about prayer. No matter how much he thought about it, prayer seemed little more than speaking into space, with his eyes closed, to someone who just wasn't there! Yet he wasn't content to leave it at that. He faced his doubt and searched for answers. He sought the help of other Christians. He read forty-three books on the subject. He checked every reference on prayer he could find in the Bible. You see, he was doubting his doubts!

The capacity to doubt is one of man's noblest powers. So it is important not to write it off or despise it. Honour it; use it; make it work for you and not against you. The Bible is a book of faith, but it is dis-armingly honest and contains testimonies of the intimate, and often agonising, struggles of those who wrestled with doubt and unbelief. Gideon, for example (Judges 6:13), had concluded that all he had been told about God was pretty suspect. Nevertheless, he struggled through his doubt and served God in such a significant way that God's people were able to live in peace for forty years because of his spiritual leadership.

Prayer reflection:
Never allow what you doubt to become your conviction. Refuse to let this happen and doubt will be defeated and prayer will become dynamic.

Day 13
REFUSAL TO GROW UP
James 4:1-10

When we admire the wisdom and insight and maturity of a young person we speak about someone having an *old* head on *young* shoulders. Much more common, however, is the opposite: a *young* head on *old* shoulders.

To grow old is not always to grow up. Sometimes this is true of spiritual life as well. Bickering, animosity, coldness towards another person let God down and show our spiritual immaturity. I think he sometimes cries out to us: 'Come on, grow up!'

James points out that the constant pursuit of personal pleasure (v 1) and an inability to identify our priorities (v 4) will stunt our growth in Jesus. These two things will be highlighted in the way we pray (vs 2, 3). First, we rush ahead, selfishly hassling God for what *we* want. If we have already decided what suits us, what's the point of praying about it? Maybe, we're afraid that if we do pray we might discover God doesn't want 'that' – and be left with a problem.

Let's learn the lesson today that God will *not* simply endorse what we've already decided. He won't throw his might behind something that is not in our best interests, or will not enrich his kingdom or fulfil his purposes. God often wants to change us, not reinforce our pride and self-centredness.

Prayer reflection:
The abuse of prayer has as profound an effect on our spiritual growth as the absence of prayer.

Day 14
BURNOUT SITUATIONS
Luke 22:39-46

Life today has been described with three words: hurry, worry and bury! An American analyst writes: 'Of the ten leading causes of death in America today, eight are attributed to stress.'

A team from the University of Manchester Institute of Science and Technology carried out a survey to ascertain the most stressful occupation in Britain. They decided, 'using their professional judgement', that the most stressful job to have was to be a coal-miner. Policemen, construction workers, aircraft pilots and prison officers followed in that order. Maybe you feel your job is top of the list!

The disciples were in burnout emotionally (v 45) and they missed the beginning of the world's salvation (vs 41-44). Jesus was clearly disappointed that their tiredness robbed him of their fellowship. After all, in trouble we want someone with us – not necessarily to do anything or to say anything, but just to be there.

It's not wrong to feel tired, but we need to organise our day so that we don't attempt to share time with God when we are too weary. Physical weariness not only robs us of reality in prayer – it can be downright dangerous (vs 40, 46)!

Prayer starter:
Father, may the pressures around and within me be a means of helping me to make time for you rather than destroying the time I need to have with you.

Hindrance busters

Complete the following:

CHALLENGE   What challenged my heart in this section more than anything is:

_____
_____
_____
_____

ENCOURAGEMENT   Looking back, what points have been a help and encouragement to praying?

_____
_____
_____
_____

ACTION   What definite steps will you take to remove hindrances to your praying?

_____
_____
_____
_____

THINK: The secret of answered prayer is to find out what God is doing – and do the same. It adds up to *five* things: *think* God's thoughts; *feel* God's emotions; *desire* God's plans; *speak* God's word; *do* God's works.

extra

Praise – there's

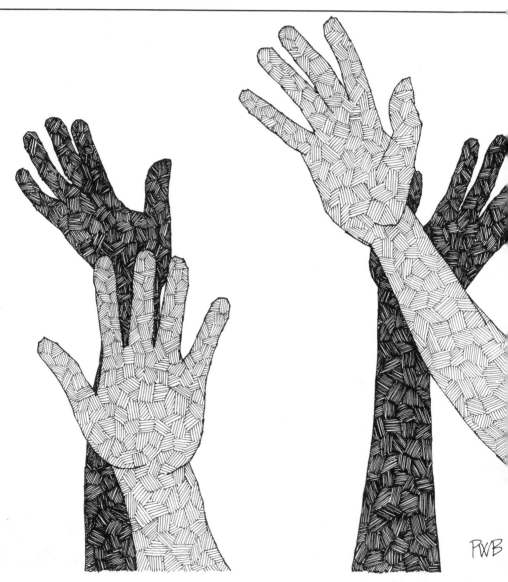

Spending half-an-hour praising God can make us feel revitalised. As growing Christians, we need to recognise the benefits on offer...

nothing like it!

Three rows from the front at our evening communion service – the focal point for the church's worship – stood Michael. As worship and praise flowed out of the congregation's heart, I could see tears on his face.

God was active in this man's life through the praise of the congregation. That night he came to my office and on his knees received Christ as Lord of his life.

GETTING STARTED

I regularly use tapes to lead me into prayer or to help me while I am praying. For years, I have used a hymn-book as I pray. The Book of *Psalms* (*especially in 'The Living Bible'*) has been a constant companion in my prayer-times. You see, the Bible says: 'Through Jesus, therefore, let us continually offer to God a sacrifice of praise – the fruit of lips that confess his name' (Hebrews 13:15).

Praise is a vital ingredient in relating to God. Have a read sometime of the *Acts of the Apostles* – particularly chapter 4. There it tells us of Peter and John who are having a hard time doing what God wanted them to do. Eventually, after a night spent in jail and then a grilling before the Sanhedrin, they get back to their Christian friends. What do they do next? They pray! Before they ever get to the point of asking for things for themselves (vs 29, 30), they pour out their praise to God.

There's nothing like praise for putting God in true perspective – seeing him as he really is. And there's nothing like having a clear view of God to make praying real. Often, when we pray, we have a big view of ourselves and a small view of God, or

a small view of ourselves and a small view of God. Sometimes, we have a small view of ourselves and such a big, gigantic view of God that we can't realistically relate to him. It helps to remember that God always wants us to have a big view of ourselves as well as a big view of him. Yes God is great, but he has also brought us into greatness, not because we deserve it, but because he is gracious to us. So we can approach him in confidence without fear, and exalt and praise his name. This will bring a real 'electricity' into praying, because with this attitude and in this climate God's presence will be obvious (Acts 4:31).

KNOWING GOD

Praise has comparatively *little* to do with hymn-books, overhead projectors, guitars, keyboards, choirs, music groups, and so on. But praise has *everything* to do with recognising the secure relationship you have with God and then making your response to him. Have a look at Psalm 150:2: 'Praise him for his acts of power; praise him for his surpassing greatness.' You see there are two things which will always help us praise God: *recognising* what God is doing and *realising* who God is; becoming aware of his conduct and his character. The person who wrote the psalm got the order right, because we tend to find it much easier to

the
prayer
principle

appreciate what someone has done than to appreciate who someone is.

It is easier for me to say to Anne, my wife: 'Thank you for that beef strogonoff – I really enjoyed it!' than it is for me to say: 'Thank you for being the kind of person you are!' But in God's eyes it's not so much what we do as who we are that is important. Of course, it is not possible to separate character from conduct, for often what a person does is because of what that person is. It's a good thing then to begin listing in our mind what God has done for us in the past and is doing for us in the present. Often that leads us on to recognise that what he does is because of who he is.

HOWEVER YOU FEEL

Sometimes, as we come to God in prayer, our praise will be *spontaneous*. That's because we feel good about God and especially close to him. Those are the times when we come to him easily and expectantly, almost as if we can't wait to get there!

A friend of mine once came out of Moorgate Underground Station in London, at three o'clock in the afternoon, singing, 'Praise my soul the King of heaven' at the top of his voice. This particular friend had just met with God in a London church.

There are times, however, when life is not like that. We are frustrated, or tired, feel life is giving us a raw deal. We may even feel critical and angry with God because of something that has happened. It's then that praise will be *sacrificial*. A sacrifice is something offered to God which costs us something. It hurts, but is offered because we really do understand who God is. This is what is called 'a sacrifice of praise'.

In a church I know, there was a lady whose little baby died completely unexpectedly. It was at the time when many Christians were singing the song 'Ascribe greatness to our God the rock.' There she was in the congregation singing: 'A God of faithfulness, without injustice, good and upright is he'… She was praising God in this way not because she felt like it but because she knew that God is *always* faithful and worthy of our praise. He never changes whether we feel like praising him or not. My 'Moorgate-Underground-singing friend' has gone through many hard, bewildering and tempestuous times since that afternoon, but he knows that God is still the same *now* as he was *then*.

After a particularly disastrous year, the prophet Habakkuk said:

'Though the fig-tree does not bud and there are no grapes on the vines, though the olive crop fails and the fields produce no food, though there are no sheep in the pen and no cattle in the stalls, yet I will rejoice in the Lord, I will be joyful in God my Saviour.' (Habakkuk 3:17, 18).

It is a good idea to read the whole of Habakkuk's prayer (chapter 3), for spontaneous or sacrificial praise will always be relevant before God. Why not make a start now – for as we have noticed it doesn't matter how we feel.

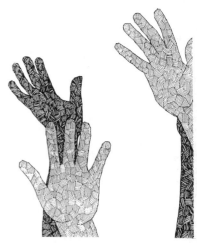

Praise – there's nothing like it!

Day 15
PRAYER PARTNERS
Psalm 34:1-3; 47:1-9

Someone once wrote:
'O crooked lonely forest tree,
And crooked because lonely,
If only comrades two or three,
Could share your lone monotony,
How very different life would be.'

That's true of life anyway, but particularly true of prayer. So many hindrances threaten our prayer life that making a commitment to one or more other people is an enormous help in praying.

Jim Elliot, a young American missionary, died trying to share the good news about Jesus with the Anca Indians (*you should read the book:* – 'Through Gates of Splendour' – *by his wife, Elizabeth*). When they married, the couple had Psalm 34:3 engraved on their wedding rings. They were more than just partners in marriage.

The heart of Christianity is about fellowship – with God, but also with others.

Think about who could be your prayer/praise partner(s). Psalm 47 brings home the impact of God's power and grace upon the nation and the need for a response *together*. We need people around us who will be positive not negative, and creative not destructive. This will both expand our horizons and minister faith into our hearts.

Prayer starter:
Lord, help me to call to mind those I could ask to be my prayer/praise partners.

Day 16
PRESCRIPTION FOR DEPRESSION
Psalm 67:1-7

One of the marks of depression in a Christian is that s/he has lost sight of who God is and what God does. In this psalm, notice that God knows what is going on. Take note that what he knows is expressed in how he rules, administers justice, and guides. He knows the end from the beginning and is perfectly able to provide for us.

In the light of all this, realise that, although we are imperfect and fail, we are created by God and for God. Remember that his forgiveness is absolute, and allow him to be God in us by the power of his Spirit.

We need to use our imagination to see ourselves being shaped by God whatever our circumstances today; to take time to write down with faith and honesty our basic life goals; to resist negative thoughts, influences, and insinuations; to begin to anticipate God's super-abundant life, spiritually, emotionally, mentally and materially; to review our priorities to see if we are really seeking God's kingdom and righteousness above all else – or if we have another agenda running; to give ourselves daily to serve other people rather than ourselves.

Having gone through this prescription, turn the encouragement in this psalm to praise God into personal experience.

Prayer starter:
Lord, turn my darkness into light, my heaviness into dancing, and my sadness into joy.

the
prayer
principle

Day 17
SERIOUS BUSINESS
Psalm 92:1-15

That brilliant Oxford scholar, C S Lewis, once said that 'Joy is the serious business of heaven'. Irrepressible joy will be the constant experience of God's people in eternity, so let's rehearse now as we realise God's constant love and faithfulness (vs 1, 2), regardless of how we feel or what we face. We should be thrilled not only by what God does, but how he thinks (vs 4, 5). Our God is never thoughtless – his mind operates before his hands.

The Salvation Army, in spite of its sterling work, has often had its critics. Someone once criticised the movement for being cheap and highly emotional. G K Chesterton defended it: 'Their methods are unassailable. Anyone who really believes in the Christian faith must do at least two things: he must dance and he must fight – dance for sheer joy and fight because he has found something that opens up the sure path to triumph.'

As you read this psalm, begin to release your praise because of the God it speaks of. Laughter and joy are never a breach of Christian good manners.

Use your mouth by 'giving thanks', 'singing', 'proclaiming'. Use your hands as well – lift them up to God. If you have an instrument, make good use of it too!

Prayer starter:
Lord, because joy is the serious business of heaven, help me to make praise a serious business on earth.

Day 18
CREATED FOR...
Psalm 104:1-35

One thing that distinguishes man from his surroundings is that he is a worshipper. We are the only living beings who can *freely* give God the worship he is looking for, although the rest of creation can and does worship him (Psalm 148). Never are we more human than when we are praising God!

Read this psalm aloud and see what happens to you! Here is ecstasy over what God has created – it is majesty and infinite variety; it is order and it is spaciousness. God deserves our praise because he is the creator.

The Hebrew word for 'created' is *bara*. Normally it is not used to describe the manufacturing of material things. In its non-biblical sense it describes the work of artists – creating a painting or a sculpture. In the Bible, the word is used exclusively for the creative work of God – creating something completely new out of nothing in an effortless way.

Nothing stimulates our praise more than seeing the greatness of God – and in spite of our smallness and sinfulness he loves us!

Prayer starter:
Help me to look around me with understanding; above me with wonder; and within me with humility; so that I might praise you.

Praise – there's nothing like it!

Day 19
INSIDE AND OUT
Psalm 118:1-16

The psalm seems to refer to a time of great national deliverance (vs 15, 16, 24), which affects the psalmist in a deeply personal way (vs 5-14). What is going on around us often affects what goes on inside us. A young airforce pilot, Christopher Benn, shot down in 1941, was eager to get back into the sky in spite of his ordeal. He said: 'Victory is not only a national affair, it is a personal matter too!'

When we see God at work on the wide canvas of history, it should affect us inside. We need to pray for evidence of God's intervention when we see the awesomeness of famine; the ruthless cruelty in the trouble-spots of the world; the sad and heart-breaking results of godlessness within our society. It's a good exercise to pray our way through the newspapers and the TV news bulletins, rather than simply discuss or criticise what we see.

The names most frequently used for God in the Old Testament are ADONAI (*his authority*); ELOHIM (*his power*); and AHWEH (*his eternity*). It is this last one which appeals to the psalmist – God has no beginning or ending; no past or future, for he is eternally present (vs 1-4). In spite of how it may look at times, God has never abandoned his creation.

Prayer starter:
As I look on the world, Lord, turn what could depress me into an opportunity to see you demonstrating your goodness and power.

Day 20
POWER UNLIMITED
Psalm 134:1-3; 135:1-21

How often we have watched the countdown at Cape Canaveral and imagined the awesome thrust of power as man blasts three-quarters of a ton of metal and instruments out of the earth's gravity-hold into space! We hardly dare to think of the progress of power since that first atom bomb fell on Hiroshima in 1945 killing 87,000 people in one second. Seven years later came the hydrogen bomb – 1,000 times stronger. Then two more years saw the first cobalt bomb being tested – 300,000 times more powerful than the hydrogen bomb.

Can we begin to visualise the power needed to get the earth into orbit or pack the sun with the energy that fills our solar system? God is a God of power unlimited (135:5-12). That's why it is important to know not only what God can do but also what he is like (135:1-4, vs 13-21). If we knew a man was going to call at our home tonight, six-foot-five in height; weighing nineteen-and-a-half stones, without an ounce of excess fat on his muscular body, and had fists like a heavyweight boxer, we would want to know if he was peaceful or violent; had a grievance against us or was coming in friendship.

Prayer starter:
Help me to grasp, Father, that your love is always backed up with your power, and your power is always tempered with your love.

the
prayer
principle

Time to...

Here are some helps for developing your friendship with God.

RELAX   Learn how to *relax* in his presence.

Sit, kneel, lie in his presence. Allow your body to express your openness to God. Unwind in his presence.

REFLECT   Learn how to *reflect* in his presence. Remember he cares for you and you are never out of his mind. Remember he loves you better than you love yourself, and accepts you as you are. So he is changing you now to be like him.

RESPOND   Learn how to *respond* in his presence. Surrender every part of yourself: your attitudes, values, thoughts, imaginations, friendships and every part of your body. Let your thoughts and plans fade and ask to see God's agenda.

REPENT   Learn how to *repent* in his presence. As you respond to him, his Spirit will 'nudge' you about areas of your life he doesn't like. Accept his verdict and repent.

RECEIVE   Learn how to *receive* in his presence. Realise he has been watching, waiting, longing, yearning to forgive, accept, embrace and set you free. Allow him to fill you with his Spirit so that you can know his joy, guidance, encouragement, power and peace.

Day 21
HANDS OUTSTRETCHED
Psalm 138:1-8

Some people struggle to believe that God has hands (vs 7, 8). They ask: 'Doesn't that reduce God to the level of man?' Yet the reverse is true – it isn't God that resembles man, but man that resembles God (Genesis 1:26).

Can you visualise today the hands of God outstretched – to welcome; to care; to provide; to protect; to hold you?

God is constant in love (v 2); he cares for the lowly (v 6); keeps us safe; opposes those who would hurt us; saves us by his power (v 7); does everything he has promised (v 8). For God not only has hands, but lips and ears (vs 3, 4).

Although the relief ship did not arrive until the 21st October, 1851, the last entry in the diary of missionary Allen Francis Gardiner, dated 5th September, read: 'Great and marvellous are the loving-kindnesses of my gracious God to me. He has preserved me hitherto, and for four days, although without bodily food, without any feelings of hunger or thirst.' The language may belong to another generation but the truth remains the same – God doesn't fail a simple and unshaken trust even though it may seem to be otherwise.

Prayer starter:
Lord, when everything seems to go wrong and my faith is weak, help me to know that you are strong and your hands are outstretched towards me.

Praise – there's nothing like it!

Prayer that strikes gold!

There's no need to panic! There's plenty of 'gold' to be had by all in the 'prayer rush'. Every Christian can experience the thrills, joys and excitements that come to determined prayer prospectors.

Prayer th

Two brothers landed in America from Europe in 1845. The older brother knew how to make sauerkraut; the younger didn't know how to make anything. Some time later the older brother joined a wagon train going West and arrived in California where he began to grow cabbages. The younger one studied metallurgy, and after some years went to California to visit his gardener brother, who was eager to show off his cabbages.

No. 2705

the prayer principle

The visitor kept looking at the ground and the gardener became irritated: 'Here I show you my fine cabbages and you have no good word to say! What's the matter with you?' The younger brother picked up a piece of stone: 'Do you know what this is?' he asked. 'It is quartz. That yellow spot is gold. You have been raising cabbages on a gold field!' And so followed one of the richest gold strikes ever made in Eldorado County.

Often we miss the richness of prayer because we do not fully realise its power. We settle for 'cabbage patch' rather than 'gold mine' prayer. In these days of constant warnings about waning energy resources - on the earth, under the earth, beneath the sea, to say nothing of pollution in the air - we need to get a hold of the inexhaustible source of infinite energy open to us through prayer. Prayer is often reduced to a necessary religious exercise which is tolerated and used to indulge our wandering thoughts. Eternal realities are allowed to become meaningless phrases and platitudes.. Eternal truth is at our fingertips and the realities of eternity within our grasp, but unthinkingly we tame down truth and dull reality.

UNLIMITED DIMENSIONS

One of the greatest threats to Christianity is neither heresy nor blasphemy but an unexciting Christian. This has nothing to do with looks, personality, temperament or ability - but everything to do with the excitement which surrounds a person who is living in the realities of another world of unlimited dimensions. He knows God loves him, and God's endless resources are available to him.

Mankind has discovered how to land people on the moon and bring them back to earth again with unbelievable timing and precision; how to climb mathematical mountains so long as the person can count to ten and possesses a calculator the size of a wrist-watch and the thickness of a credit card; how to perform medical miracles by replacement and transplant surgery; how to pierce the walls of outer space, land machines on Mars, and shrink our world until every continent is only a few hours away. But over all of these projects and achievements is the word - LIMITED! The tragedy is we settle for the best this world has to give and fail to take advantage of the best God has to give.

Yet the power-package of prayer is unbelievable. Again and again in the Bible, we are invited to use and experience the power of the name of Jesus - look up and investigate Luke 9:1 with Luke 10:17; now check out Mark 16:17, 18; think about Acts 3:6 and Acts 3:16; consider what's going on in Acts 8:26, 27. All magnificent stuff! It is no magic formula tacked on

t strikes gold!

to the end of a prayer when we pray 'in Jesus' Name'.

In many lands it is customary for a married woman to take the name of her husband – legally she is placed under his care and authority. For the sake of illustration, let's suppose that the bride is very poor in every way. She has no money in the bank or building society; no property; no borrowing earning power; no record of any worth at all. Let's suppose that her husband *has* and *is* all that she *hasn't* and *isn't*. The moment she becomes 'Mrs' she moves out of the past poverty and powerlessness into all that the name of her husband means. She no longer acts in *her* name but in his. She can spend money from his bank; live securely in any property he owns; operate comfortably on his borrowing power; enjoy his earnings; and live in the splendour of all that he is worth.

Now think about how the church is betrothed to becomes Mrs Jesus! She is totally authorised to operate in the name of Jesus.

I realise this is a poor illustration and wide open to all kinds of criticism, but I'm trying to convey the limitless resources of praying in the name of Jesus. Perhaps equally impoverished is the illustration of the power of attorney – a legal arrangement whereby one person can represent another in his absence in certain, or in all, matters. In our fellowship, we have a number of people who serve Jesus in his church overseas and so are out of the country for long periods. There are those left behind, who have power of attorney for them while they are gone – in their absence they are authorised to act on their behalf regarding their finances, their property, and other personal issues. Jesus has given every believer unlimited and general power of attorney in all matters, and with this is the right to use his Name in every situation. What power! The sky is the limit? Not so, there are no limits!

IN FOCUS

We need to take seriously John 14:13, 14. Ask God to give you greater understanding of what Jesus is teaching here in these final hours before his sacrifice on the cross. There are four things that every Christian needs to hold constantly in focus:

1   The Spiritual life of any Christian will never rise above the level of his praying. What a Christian is before God in prayer, that he is.

2   The ultimate effectiveness of any church will never rise above the level of the combined prayer-life of its members.

3   The corporate prayer of any church will never be greater than the personal prayer-lives of those who are in membership.

4   The Christian's prayer-life will never rise above the level of his own personal, regular time of worship with God.

Stop for a moment and read these statements aloud. Check out their truth. Then, hold them firmly in focus.

Move on now to our next Bible selection and allow God's word to speak to you about his power in prayer.

the
prayer
principle

Day 22
GET GOING
Daniel 6:1-16

the
prayer
principle

Darius was invited to become God for thirty days (v 7) and he fell for it! Daniel kept on doing what he had always done (*as regularly as his morning coffee; afternoon tea; and hot drink at bed-time!*) regardless of the pressures (v 10). He knew where the real power lay – not with governments or palaces but with the one who is on the throne of heaven. He knew that prayer is not so much *me* bringing God into *my* world to solve *my* problems as it is *God* bringing me into *his* world to serve *his* purposes.

For prayer touches three worlds at the same time and does so immediately. It touches heaven – for it touches God as nothing else can, and releases his power as nothing else will. It touches earth – for it affects man at a depth and a reality he is not even aware of. It touches hell – for it disturbs and disrupts the devil's activity more than any other human enterprise.

Did you notice it was the king who was trapped, not Daniel, and that it was the king who really struggled with what was happening (v 14), not Daniel? Trauma, anxiety, intrigue and plotting were all going on around Daniel but he remained peaceful as he prayed. He was the one who knew where the real power lay.

Prayer starter:
Help me, Lord, to recognise your true power. Make me so secure in this that I don't feel the need to promote myself or manipulate others in order to do your will

Day 23
FACE THE TEST
Daniel 6:17-28

The great preacher Charles Spurgeon once said the reason the lions didn't eat Daniel was that he was 'mostly backbone and the rest was grit'! That's not what Daniel says: 'God sent his angel' (v 22) – presumably in response to his panic-proof prayers.

Today we relegate angels to nativity plays and Christmas greetings cards. Then we put them away with the rest of the decorations until the next year. However, we're not dealing with irrelevant, beautiful, song-singing, trumpet-playing, innocuous beings – but with the powerful servants of God.

Jesus was well aware of angels around him from his birth to his ascension. The only time they seemed to have been missing was when he hung on the cross – then he experienced utter and complete aloneness.

Accordng to the Bible, angels are superior to humans in strength, beauty and intelligence, but inferior to God who created them. They are countless in number and very powerful. One of the Old Testament prophets tells us that 186,000 foot soldiers are no match for one angel. They were certainly effective in the lions' den protecting a faithful man whose witness affected four emperors and penetrated two mighty pagan empires.

Prayer starter:
Make me aware, Lord, of the heavenly hosts I cannot see. Help me to believe that prayer causes you to despatch these messengers into situations I cannot handle alone

Prayer that strikes gold!

Day 24
TAP IN TO...
Colossians 1:3-14

It's one thing to know what to do, but a completely different thing being able to do it. Often our problem as Christians is not ignorance but disobedience. Disobedience, which is often caused because we do not believe we have the ability to carry out what we know God wants, and that unbelief and fear paralyses us. Yet God offers us power as well as pardon.

During the General Strike of 1926, many people in my native Lanarkshire scrabbled on the coal bins gathering little fragments that had been thrown away as useless, while beneath them were great seams of coal waiting to be mined. Often we restrict ourselves to 'surface' prayers, ignoring the 'hidden' untapped resources of power just waiting to be released.

Paul prayed that the Colossians might have great endurance. Not simply the ability to let the tide of events flow over them, but the ability to deal triumphantly with anything that life could do to them. The patience he prayed for is a quality of mind and heart which enables us to deal with unpleasantness, maliciousness and cruelty, without bitterness; to deal with unteachableness, without despair; and to deal with foolishness, without irritation. The joy he prayed for is a radiant attitude to life, regardless of circumstances.

Prayer starter:
Father, help me to tap into your resources. Help me to exchange *my* poverty for *your* power

Day 25
OPPORTUNITY KNOCKS
Colossians 4:2-4

The escapologist, Houdini, who used to release himself from ropes, chains, padlocks, sacks, boxes and so on, was defeated once. Placed in a prison cell, he worked hard to pick the lock in the set time, but was defeated by the clock. Only afterwards did he discover that the cell door had been unlocked! All the time he had been trying to do what was already done.

Here Paul is aware that it is *God* who unlocks doors – often by prayer. Our part is to make good use of the opportunities that God gives. For Paul, it was the opportunity to tell others about the wonders of salvation (v 3). What will you do with the 'opportunities' God gives you today?

Years ago, during the construction of one of the East River bridges in New York, engineers were baffled by an old sunken barge which lay embedded on the river-bottom. Powerful engines, steel cables, derricks and rafts failed to remove the obstruction. Then a young man, fresh from technical college, was given permission to try his hand. At low tide he had a large barge towed out to the spot and each end fastened to the sunken wreck. As the tide came in so the barge rose, bringing with it the submerged wreck. The young engineer had harnessed the limitless power of the ocean tides.

Prayer starter:
Prayer unlocks and harnesses God's limitless power. Thank him for opening the door for you. Then trust his power when opportunity knocks

the
prayer
principle

Prayer that strikes gold!

Day 26
HELP AT HAND
Romans 8:26, 27

When we pray we have two helpers: Jesus is helping us in heaven; the Holy Spirit is helping us on earth. We need to learn how to trust the Holy Spirit to influence our minds – by giving us *right* thoughts, *right* impressions, *right* burdens as we pray. He will always help us to pray in the will of the Father, for the glory of the Son, and by the guidelines of the Bible.

However, he not only wants to influence our minds, he also wants to influence our mouths! Often we run out of words when we are praying, that's when we need to allow the Spirit to help us (vs 26, 27).

Often we don't know how to pray for people or situations either because the situation is too complex, or because we feel there is much which is positive and negative on both sides. What can we do? Allow the Spirit to take control.

What will it be like? Sometimes it will sound like groaning; sometimes like sighing; sometimes like weeping; and sometimes like a language we have never learned. This is not hysteria or emotionalism – it is allowing God to be God in us and through us.

Prayer starter:
Forgive me, Father, that sometimes I have found praying dull and boring. Help me to enter into the magnificence of the open door of prayer

Day 27
ALLOW GOD TO BE GOD
Psalm 119:33-40

This, the longest psalm in the Bible, is a series of eight-line meditations based on the twenty-two letters of the Hebrew alphabet. It celebrates that each fresh word from God reveals the author not just information. As God gives us knowledge of his power in our lives in a small way, so he puts a small test before us. As soon as we discover that God's power is real and effective in that way, then we are made aware that his power is every bit as effective in a bigger test.

Breeding atomic fuel works in the same way. Natural uranium contains only 0.7% of fissionable U-235. Nearly all the rest of it is non-fissionable U-238. But when U-235 splits in two and produces heat, it also yields free neutrons. Some of these are needed to keep the reaction going; they make other U-235 atoms split. Some neutrons escape or are absorbed by structural materials in the reactor. The rest of the neutrons enter the nuclei of the U-238 atoms and make them turn into plutonium, which is just as fissionable as U-235 and can be used as atomic fuel.

The importance of this development can only be realised if we consider that one pound of uranium has been the equivalent of about 18,200 lbs of coal: under the new process the same pound of uranium would be equivalent to 2,600,000 lbs of coal.

God has organised the Christian life on the principal of the breeder reactor – we begin with something very small but as we allow God to be God in that it expands.

Prayer that strikes gold!

Day 28
LOOK ON THE BRIGHT SIDE
Psalm 86:1-7

Years ago a minister in Philadelphia was walking in the slum area of the city when a boy of about six came out of a dairy carrying a jug of milk. He was walking very carefully, but still he slipped and fell. The little boy was distraught, not because he had spilled the milk, but because he had broken the jug – punishment was just around the corner!

Harry Moorehouse, the minister, tried to put the jug together again. After one or two failures, finally the jug was complete, except for the handle. Harry handed the handle to the boy who poked it toward the place it belonged and knocked the whole thing apart again. This time there was no stopping the tears.

Moorehouse gathered the boy in his arms; took him to a crockery store; bought a brand new jug; went to the dairy and had it filled with milk. 'Now' he said, 'will your mother smack you?' 'Aw, no sir because it's a lot better jug than we had before!'

David, who wrote today's psalm, knew there was no point in trying to patch the pieces of his life together, so he cried out to God for help. He was aware of his need (v 1) but he was also aware that God is 'kind and forgiving' (v 5).

How confident are you today in your God?

Prayer starter:

Help me, Lord, to dismiss any negative thoughts I have of you, so that I can be free to come to you as you really are – a good God

Get rich!

THINK THROUGH 'Satan dreads nothing but prayer. His one concern is to keep the saints from praying. He fears nothing from prayerless studies; prayerless work; prayerless religion. He laughs at our toil, mocks our wisdom, but trembles when we pray.'   *Samuel Chadwick*

'I fear the prayers of John Knox more than I fear all the armies on the face of the earth.'

Mary, Queen of Scots

PRAYER BREAKERS
1   A selfish purpose – James 4:3.
2   Sin undealt with – Psalm 66:18; 139:23, 24; Isaiah 59:1, 2.
3   Idols in the heart – (*things that take God's place*) – Ezekiel 14:3.
4   Lack of concern for others – Proverbs 21:13; Luke 6:38; 1 John 3:22.
5   An unforgiving spirit – Matthew 11:25.
6   A wrong relationship between husband/wife – 1 Peter 3:7.
7   Unbelief – James 1:5-7.
8   Satanic opposition – Ephesians 6:10-13.

Are there things I need to put right?

TIME FOR GOD   In a 168 hour week how much of that time am I prepared to devote to prayer? How will I distribute that time throughout the week?

extra

WHAT NEXT!

You've finished this book. What are you going to do about Bible reading now? Well, for a start, there are four other *Growing with Jesus* books. If you have already worked through all of those, Scripture Union offers a choice of three different styles of notes for adults. One of them should suit you!

You may order GWJ books and Scripture Union notes from
● your local Christian bookshop ● your Scripture Union church representative
● by post from Scripture Union Mail order.

SU ADULT BIBLE READING NOTES

DAILY BREAD Practical help from the Bible for everyday Christian living. £1.60 quarterly

ALIVE TO GOD Bible exploration for living by the Spirit. £1.60 quarterly

DAILY NOTES An in-depth reflection for more experienced Bible readers. £1.60 quarterly

GROWING WITH JESUS SERIES

the ME problem by Rob Warner

the LOVE story by Lynn Green

the POWER dimension by Michael Cole

the GOD slot by Philip Mohabir

the PRAYER principle by Jim Graham

- -

ORDER FORM

To: Scripture Union Mail Order, 9-11 Clothier Road, Bristol BS4 5RL
Tel: (0272) 719709 24 hr order line Fax: (0272) 711472

GWJ Books	Total		Quantity	Price
Me problem (£2.25*)	_____	Daily Bread (£9.20*)	_____	
Love Story (£2.25*)	_____	Daily Notes (£9.20*)	_____	
Power dimension (£2.25*)	_____	Alive to God (£9.20*)	_____	
God slot (£2.25*)	_____	**Total**		
Prayer principle (£2.25*)	_____			

*Including UK postage and packing. (*Payment with order please*)

Please send me one year's supply of the above notes starting

☐ **January** ☐ **April** ☐ **July** ☐ **October** (*please tick one*)

Overseas rates Europe +£1.50 per subscription. Outside Europe +£3.00 per subscription.
PLEASE USE BLOCK CAPITALS

Name _____

Address _____

_____ Postcode _____

I enclose CHEQUE/POSTAL ORDER amount £ _____

Please debit my ACCESS/BARCLAYCARD amount £ _____

| | | | | | | | | | | | | | | | | | | Expiry date | | | | |

In **Australia**, write for subscription details to: Scripture Union, 241 Flinders Lane, Melbourne, Vic 3000.
In **USA**, write for subscription details to: Scripture Union, 7000 Ludlow Street, Upper Darby, PA 19082.
In **Canada**, write for subscription details to: Scripture Union, 1885 Clements Road, Unit 226, Pickering,
Ontario, L1W 3V4. In **South Africa**, write for subscription details to: Scripture Union, Millard House,
Camp Ground Road, Rondebosch 7700.

GWJ94